MAKE 2024
YOUR YEAR

Make 2024 Your Year

Poetry Affirmations for Success

Walter the Educator™

SKB

Silent King Books a WhichHead Imprint

dedicated to everyone in search of
success

CONTENTS

WHY I CREATED THIS BOOK?

Creating a poetry book that motivates a person to achieve success can be a powerful tool for inspiration and personal growth. Poetry has a unique ability to touch the depths of our emotions and convey complex ideas in a concise and beautiful manner. By combining motivational themes with poetic expression, this book can provide encouragement, guidance, and a sense of purpose to readers. It can help individuals overcome obstacles; stay focused on their goals, and remind them of the resilience and determination needed to achieve success. Through the power of words, this poetry book can inspire and empower individuals to reach their highest potential.

ONE

SO GO FORTH

In the depths of your soul, lies the fire's embrace,
A desire to conquer, with strength and with grace,
For success awaits, in the distant unknown,
A journey untrodden, a path yet unshown.

With every step forward, you'll face trials and fears,
But remember, my friend, you're stronger than your tears,
For within you resides an unwavering might,
A spirit that's destined to rise to the height.

Embrace every challenge, with courage and zeal,
Let passion guide you, let your heart fully feel,
The power that lies within your very core,
To achieve greatness, and so much more.

Though obstacles may come, like storms in the night,
Hold onto your dreams, keep them burning so bright,

For success is not measured by wealth or by fame,
But by the strength of your will, and the fire in your name.
So dare to dream big, reach for the stars,
Let no one tell you what's within or what's ours,
For you hold the key to unlock your own fate,
To conquer the world, and to celebrate.
Believe in yourself, let your spirit take flight,
And let the passion within you ignite,
For success is not far, it's within your reach,
So go forth, my dear, and let your dreams teach.

TWO

SIDE BY SIDE

In the realm of dreams, where greatness lies,
A fire burns within, ready to rise.
Embrace the challenges that come your way,
For they shape your character day by day.
Success is not measured by wealth or fame,
But by the strength of will, burning like a flame.
Follow your passion, let it be your guide,
And let your heart soar, spreading its wings wide.
Dream big, my friend, reach for the stars above,
Unlock your fate, with unwavering love.
For in the depths of your soul, a power resides,
Waiting to be unleashed, to conquer tides.
Believe in yourself, for you hold the key,
To unlock the door to the person you'll be.
Let not fear nor doubt cloud your mind,
For within you, a champion you'll find.

With each step forward, you'll grow and learn,
Through every failure, your spirit will burn.
So rise, my friend, let your dreams take flight,
And paint the canvas of your life, bold and bright.
　　Success is not a destination reached,
But a journey embraced, passion unleashed.
So let your dreams be the winds that guide,
And with perseverance, you'll soar, side by side.

THREE

FOREVER STRONG

In the depths of your heart, where dreams reside,
A fire burns, a flame you cannot hide.
Embrace the challenges, they're your stepping stones,
For through them, success you shall own.
Unleash your passion, let it guide your way,
In pursuit of greatness, each and every day.
For it's the fuel that ignites your soul,
Leading you towards your ultimate goal.
Believe in yourself, for you hold the key,
To unlock the doors of possibility.
With unwavering faith and strength untold,
You'll conquer mountains, no matter how bold.
Let failure be your teacher, not your foe,
For in its lessons, your wisdom will grow.
With resilience and courage, you'll rise above,
Embracing the journey, the push and the shove.

Success is not a destination, my friend,
But a journey that seems to have no end.
So cherish each step, both big and small,
For they're the building blocks of your rise to the call.
Let your spirit soar, let your dreams take flight,
For within you lies a power, shining so bright.
Embrace the challenges, follow your heart's song,
And success will be yours, forever strong.

FOUR

SHINING BRIGHT

In the depths of your soul, a fire burns bright,
A passion that yearns to take flight.
Embrace the challenges that come your way,
For they will shape you, come what may.

Success is not found in the easy road,
But in the trials that make you grow.
Let not fear or doubt hold you back,
In the face of adversity, stay on track.

Believe in yourself, with unwavering trust,
For within you lies the power, the lust,
To achieve greatness, to reach new heights,
To conquer the darkness, embrace the light.

The journey may be long, with twists and turns,
But with each step, a lesson to learn.
Cherish the moments, both big and small,
For they are the building blocks of it all.

So, dream big and chase your desires,
Let passion fuel you, let it inspire.
With determination and courage, you'll find,
That success is yours, just a matter of time.

For in the depths of your soul, you hold the key,
To unlock a world where dreams become reality.
Embrace the challenges, believe in your might,
And success will be yours, shining bright.

FIVE

LET YOUR SPIRIT SHINE

In the realm where dreams reside,
A fire burns deep inside,
A yearning to break free,
And find the person they're meant to be.
Embrace the challenges that come your way,
For they are the stepping stones that pave your way,
In every stumble and fall,
Lies the strength to conquer it all.
Believe in yourself, oh mighty soul,
Let not doubt take its toll,
For within you lies the power,
To climb the highest tower.
Success is not a distant shore,
But a journey to adore,

Each step, a lesson to learn,
Each obstacle, a chance to discern.
 Follow the beat of your own drum,
Let your passion guide you, overcome,
In every path you choose to tread,
Find joy in the journey ahead.
 For life's truest treasures lie,
Not in the end, but as time flies,
Embrace the challenges, believe in your might,
And cherish every moment, day and night.
 So go forth, my dear friend,
With courage, your heart to lend,
In the pursuit of dreams untold,
Let your spirit shine, unfold.

SIX

ACHIEVE THE SUCCESS

In the face of challenges, don't despair,
For success lies within, if you dare.
Embrace the unknown, with passion ignite,
And let your spirit soar, take flight.
The path may be winding, treacherous, and steep,
But deep within, your dreams you must keep.
Believe in yourself, in your heart's true desire,
And let the flames of ambition burn higher.
Unlock the potential that lies deep within,
Let your determination be your greatest weapon.
For greatness awaits those who dare to dream,
And success is born from the courage to scheme.
In the darkest hours, when doubts arise,
Remember your purpose, let it energize.
Trust in your abilities, both big and small,
And conquer the obstacles, standing tall.

So don't be afraid to chase after your dreams,
For nothing is impossible, so it seems.
Believe in yourself, your power and might,
And success will be yours, shining bright.
In this vast universe, you hold the key,
To unlock the door to the person you can be.
Embrace the challenges, with passion ignite,
And achieve the success you've always held in sight.

SEVEN

YOU'LL REACH THE TOP

In the depths of your soul, a fire burns bright,
A yearning for greatness, a beacon of light.
Let not doubt cloud your mind, nor fear hold you back,
For success lies within you, stay on the right track.
Embrace the challenges, they make you grow,
Each obstacle faced, an opportunity to know,
That strength resides in you, untapped and strong,
Unleash your potential, let it carry you along.
The journey of success is not for the faint-hearted,
It demands resilience, for it cannot be charted.
With every step forward, you learn and evolve,
Failure is but a teacher, helping problems to solve.
Let your dreams be your compass, guiding your way,
Fueling your passion, each and every day.

Believe in yourself, for you hold the key,
To unlock your greatness, to set yourself free.
Success is not a destination, but a lifelong quest,
Embrace the process, give it your very best.
Trust in your abilities, let your spirit soar,
For within you lies greatness, forevermore.
So be fearless in pursuing your dreams,
Embrace the challenges, no matter how extreme.
With perseverance and faith, you'll reach the top,
And in the end, success will never stop.

EIGHT

EMBRACE THE FIGHT

In the depths of your soul, a fire burns bright,
Igniting the spirit with its radiant light.
A power within, waiting to be released,
A force that can conquer and never be ceased.
Embrace the challenges that come your way,
For they are the stepping stones to a brighter day.
With every obstacle, you grow stronger still,
Unleashing the potential that lies within your will.
Dream big, dear soul, and reach for the sky,
Let not the limitations make your dreams shy.
For greatness resides in the depths of your heart,
Unleash your passion, let it set you apart.
Believe in yourself, for no one else can,
You hold the key to your destiny's plan.
With every step forward, you'll find your way,
Success is not a destination, but a journey, they say.

Cherish the moments, both big and small,
For they shape your story, they make it all.
The road may be winding, with twists and turns,
But with perseverance, your flame brightly burns.
So rise, dear soul, and embrace the fight,
Let your spirit soar, reach astonishing heights.
Success is not measured by wealth or acclaim,
But by the joy and fulfillment in your own name.

NINE

TO CONQUER MOUNTAINS

In the face of challenges, we shall stand,
With unwavering strength, we'll take command.
For success is not the absence of strife,
But the journey we live, embracing life.
    Each obstacle is a chance to grow,
To learn, to adapt, to let our spirits glow.
For it's in the flames of adversity's fire,
That we find our true selves, our deepest desire.
    Embrace the storms that come your way,
They'll shape your character, come what may.
For success is not a fleeting prize,
But the wisdom gained as we rise.
    Cherish every moment, both good and bad,
For they're the building blocks of the life we've had.

For in each step, we find our strength,
And in each breath, our life's true length.
    So let us strive, with hearts ablaze,
To conquer mountains, to walk through maze.
For success is not a destination to reach,
But a lifelong quest, within our reach.

TEN

UNIMAGINABLE HEIGHTS

In the depths of the unknown, where challenges reside,
A flame of determination, burning deep inside.
Embrace the trials that come, with an unwavering heart,
For it is through adversity, true greatness will impart.
Believe in your own power, let doubt be cast away,
Unleash the strength within, let it guide you every day.
For success is not a fleeting moment, a destination to attain,
But a lifelong journey, where growth and lessons reign.
Cherish every step you take, every hurdle you surmount,
For it is in those moments, true fulfillment can be

found.

The path may be uncertain, the road may seem unclear,

But trust in your abilities, and fearlessly persevere.

Unlock the greatness that lies within, let your dreams take flight,

With passion as your compass, you'll reach unimaginable heights.

For success is not defined by accolades or wealth,

But by the joy and purpose found in pursuing oneself.

So embrace the challenges, with a spirit bold and strong,

For they are the stepping stones to where you truly belong.

Believe in your own journey, for it is uniquely yours,

And let the pursuit of success be an endless source of allure.

ELEVEN

FEARLESSLY PERSEVERE

In the tapestry of life, woven with care,
There lies a path, beyond compare.
A journey untrodden, yet to be sought,
Where dreams take flight, and battles are fought.
Embrace the challenges, they hold the key,
To unlock the greatness that lies within thee.
For success is not found in accolades and praise,
But in the strength gained through life's turbulent maze.
Believe in yourself, for you hold the power,
To conquer the obstacles that come by the hour.
With every setback, a lesson to learn,
To grow and evolve, as the tides of life turn.
Find joy in the process, the ups and the downs,
For they shape your character, like gems in the

ground.
It's not about reaching the pinnacle's peak,
But about the person you become, as you seek.
    So cherish each moment, both big and small,
For they paint the canvas of your life's call.
Success is not measured by wealth or fame,
But by the fulfillment you find on this beautiful game.
    You have the fire, the passion, the drive,
To create a life where dreams come alive.
Embrace the challenges, fearlessly persevere,
For they lead to purpose, to belonging, my dear.

TWELVE

EVERY STEP YOU TAKE

In the realm of dreams, where ambitions reside,
A spirit awakened, ready to stride.
With fiery heart and a determined mind,
Embrace the challenges, leave no fear behind.
Success, like a beacon, calls from afar,
But the journey itself is the brightest star.
For in the pursuit of dreams, we discover,
The strength within, the will to uncover.
Each step, a lesson, a chance to grow,
In every setback, a chance to know,
That failure's embrace is not a defeat,
But a stepping stone to victory, sweet.
Find joy in the process, the highs and lows,
For it is in the struggle true greatness shows.
Embrace the uncertainties, the unknown,
For in those moments, your true self is known.

Success is not found in the destination alone,
But in the transformation, the seeds that are sown.
So let your spirit soar, unfettered and free,
Embrace the challenges, let your heart be the key.

With unwavering faith in your own ability,
You'll rise above, with unwavering agility.
For success is not measured by fame or wealth,
But by the journey, the growth and the self.

So, dreamer, hold tight to your vision true,
Embrace the challenges, let them guide you.
For success awaits, in every step you take,
Embrace the journey, and let your spirit awake.

THIRTEEN

LIFE OF FULFILLMENT

In the realm of dreams, where possibilities reside,
A spark ignites, deep within, where passions hide.
Embrace the challenges that come your way,
For in the face of adversity, you shall find your sway.
    Success, oh sweet success, a siren's call,
Beckoning you to rise, to stand tall.
Not measured in wealth or fleeting fame,
But in the growth achieved, in life's intricate game.
    Cherish each moment, for time is a precious gift,
In the pursuit of success, let not your spirit drift.
For it's not the destination, but the journey you embrace,
That paints the canvas of your life with grace.
    Unlock the greatness that lies within,
With unwavering belief, let your journey begin.

Fear not the unknown, for it holds your key,
To a life of fulfillment, where you truly can be free.
   Trust in your abilities, let your passion guide,
With every step you take, let your dreams collide.
For success is not a destination, but a state of mind,
A culmination of effort, where purpose you find.
   So, rise with determination, let your spirit soar,
Achieve success on your own terms, and forevermore,
Remember, my friend, it's not in the accolades you receive,
But in the joy found in the pursuit, where true success will cleave.

FOURTEEN

OVERCOMING PAINS

In the realm of dreams, where hope resides,
A journey awaits, where success abides.
With every step, a challenge we face,
Embracing the unknown, with strength and grace.
    Through trials and tribulations we grow,
Unfolding our wings, ready to show,
That in the face of adversity's might,
We find our true selves, shining so bright.
    Success is not merely a destination,
But a state of being, a transformation.
It lies not in trophies or worldly gains,
But in the joy of overcoming pains.
    Each moment cherished, like gems in a crown,
For in the pursuit, our purpose is found.
With passion as our compass, we navigate,
Through stormy seas and paths that oscillate.

So let us not fear the path unknown,
For therein lies the seeds we've sown.
In the embrace of challenges, we find,
The strength to rise and leave no dream behind.
Success is not a singular event,
But a lifelong journey, a testament.
To the power within, waiting to ignite,
And illuminate our spirits, shining bright.

FIFTEEN

SUCCESS IS YOURS

In the realm of dreams, where magic lies,
A spirit soars and reaches the skies.
Embrace the challenges, they are your guide,
To unlock the greatness you hold inside.

With every step, a new path unfolds,
A story written, waiting to be told.
Trust in your abilities, let them shine,
For success is yours, and it's divine.

The journey may be long, filled with doubt,
But every moment is what life's about.
Cherish each moment, both big and small,
For in their embrace, you'll find it all.

Success is not measured by wealth or fame,
But by the joy and fulfillment you claim.
It lies in the pursuit of your own dreams,
In the laughter that echoes, in silent streams.

So let your spirit soar, like a bird in flight,
Conquer the challenges with all your might.
Believe in yourself, and the path you tread,
For success is yours, just ahead.

In the tapestry of life, you'll find your place,
A purpose discovered, a life to embrace.
Embrace the uncertainties, let them be,
For in transformation, success you'll see.

So take a leap of faith, and trust the way,
The universe will guide you, day by day.
Cherish each step, as you journey on,
For success is found, when fears are gone.

In the pursuit of dreams, you'll find your bliss,
A life well-lived, a sweet, eternal kiss.
Embrace the challenges, let your spirit soar,
For success is yours, now and evermore.

SIXTEEN

DARE TO DREAM

In the dance of life, uncertainties lie,
A path unknown, where dreams amplify,
Embrace the unknown, let fears subside,
For success awaits on the other side.
The journey unfolds, like a tale untold,
Where challenges arise, and stories unfold,
In every step taken, strength is found,
And the soul discovers its purpose profound.
Success is not a destination to reach,
But a transformation that words can't teach,
It's the growth that happens within the soul,
As we navigate through life's ebb and flow.
Let go of doubts, and let passion ignite,
For success is born in the heart's pure light,
Embrace the uncertainties, with open arms,
And witness the magic that life's journey charms.

For in every stumble, a lesson is learned,
And with every failure, a new way is earned,
Success is not a trophy, nor a prize to attain,
But the joy found in the pursuit, amidst the rain.
So dare to dream, and dare to strive,
For success is the fire that keeps us alive,
In the dance of life, let your spirit soar,
And success will find you, forevermore.

SEVENTEEN

A STORY TO UNFOLD

In life's vast tapestry, a quest unfolds,
Where dreams and aspirations take their hold.
Success, a beacon in the distance gleams,
Yet not defined by wealth or worldly schemes.
Embrace the challenges, let them ignite,
A fire within, a burning, fierce delight.
For in the face of trials, true strength is found,
And growth emerges from uncertain ground.
Measure not success by medals or acclaim,
But by the lessons learned and goals reclaimed.
The journey, rich with twists and turns untold,
Is where fulfillment lies, a story to unfold.
Find joy in moments, small and grand alike,
In every step, a victory takes its strike.
For success resides not in the final prize,
But in the soul awakened, reaching for the skies.

So let each day be filled with purpose true,
And let your dreams guide every step you do.
No path too steep, no challenge too immense,
For within you lies the power to commence.
Success is not a destination sought,
But a state of being, a mindset taught.
Embrace the adventure, let your spirit soar,
And success, dear friend, shall forever be yours.

EIGHTEEN

STATE OF MIND

In the realm of uncertainty, where challenges reside,
Lies the path to success, where dreams truly collide.
For success is not measured by accolades or fame,
But by the fire within, that burns like a flame.
Embrace the unknown, let it be your guide,
For in the face of adversity, greatness resides.
Obstacles may seem daunting, but fear not their might,
For they are mere stepping stones, leading to the light.
Success is not a destination, but a state of mind,
A journey of growth, where treasures you'll find.
Believe in yourself, trust the path you tread,
With passion and perseverance, your spirit will spread.
Let go of doubts, let your dreams take flight,
For in the pursuit of passion, you'll find pure delight.
It's not about the destination, but the joy in the

chase,
The lessons learned, the hurdles you embrace.
 So rise above the noise, let your spirit soar,
Unleash your potential, like never before.
Success is within you, waiting to be unfurled,
Embrace the uncertainties and conquer the world.

NINETEEN

JOY CAN BE FOUND

In the depths of a dream, where hope resides,
Lies the fire that burns, where success hides.
It's not in the accolades or grand acclaim,
But in the journey, where we carve our name.
Success is not a destination to attain,
But a state of mind, where dreams remain.
It's not in the riches or the fame we seek,
But in the lessons learned, when we're feeling weak.
When faced with challenges, don't despair,
For they are the stones on the path to where
You'll find your purpose, your true calling,
In the face of uncertainty, keep on falling.
Believe in yourself, trust the path you tread,
For success is not measured by what lies ahead.
It's in the courage to chase your desires,
And the strength to rise when your spirit tires.

So let your passion guide you, like a guiding star,
And let your determination carry you far.
Embrace the failures, learn from each mistake,
For it's in those moments, true success will awake.

So don't be disheartened by the twists and turns,
For in the pursuit of your dreams, the fire burns.
Success is not a destination to be found,
But a journey of growth, where joy can be found.

TWENTY

SUCCESS BLOOMS BRIGHTEST

In the depths of doubt, where shadows creep,
A fire within, a dream to keep.
Embrace the challenges that lie ahead,
For within them lies the path to tread.

Success, a journey, not a destination,
A symphony of trials and tribulations.
Through valleys low and mountains high,
We find our purpose, we learn to fly.

Believe in yourself, let doubts dissolve,
Unleash the power, let problems evolve.
For in the face of uncertainty's gaze,
We find the strength to navigate life's maze.

Success is not defined by worldly might,
Nor by the treasures we amass in sight.

But by the growth that blooms within,
And the passion that sets our souls to spin.

Let failures be the stepping stones,
Upon which resilience truly hones.
With each setback, rise and try again,
For it is through persistence, we attain.

Trust the path you tread, with steady stride,
Embrace the uncertainties, let them guide.
For success is a state of mind, you see,
A mindset that sets your spirit free.

So let go of doubts, embrace the unknown,
Unleash the power that's uniquely your own.
For in the pursuit of your heartfelt dreams,
Success blooms brightest, or so it seems.

TWENTY-ONE

DANCE OF LIFE

On the path to success, we embark,
A journey filled with light and dark.
With every step, we strive to be,
The best version of you and me.
Embrace the challenges, embrace the pain,
For they are the stepping stones to gain.
In the face of uncertainty, we find,
Strength and courage deep inside.
Success is not a destination to reach,
But a journey that teaches and enrich.
It's not measured by fame or wealth,
But by the growth of heart and health.
In the pursuit of dreams, we soar,
Opening new doors, forevermore.
With passion as our guiding star,
We rise above all limits, near and far.

Believe in yourself, and you will see,
The power to shape your destiny.
For success is not defined by others,
But by the love and joy it smothers.
So keep pushing forward, never relent,
With every setback, be resilient.
For in the face of adversity,
We find the true meaning of victory.
Together we stand, united we thrive,
In this grand symphony called life.
Embrace the journey, embrace the strife,
And success will be ours, in this dance of life.

TWENTY-TWO

EMBRACE THE UNCERTAINTY

In the realm of dreams, where stars reside,
There lies a path for those who stride.
Success, my friend, is not a prize,
Of worldly goods or fleeting highs.

For true success, it's not the wealth,
But growth and passion, inner health.
A journey unique, yours to unfold,
A story written, yet untold.

Seek not the fame, the glitz, the show,
But let your heart and soul bestow,
The gift of purpose, burning bright,
Igniting dreams, a radiant light.

In every step, in every try,
In every tear, in every sigh,

You'll find the strength to carry on,
To rise above, until you've won.

For success is not a fixed terrain,
But a spirit that can't be restrained.
It's found in failures, lessons learned,
In every bridge that you have burned.

So let your heart be bold and free,
Embrace the uncertainty,
For in the quest to find your way,
You'll discover who you are, each day.

Success is not defined by others' eyes,
But by the joy it brings, the love it ties.
So chase your dreams, my friend, with all your might,
And success will find you, in the darkest night.

TWENTY-THREE

SOUL FOREVER CHANGED

In the realm of dreams, where passions ignite,
A journey unfolds, bathed in golden light.
Success, dear friend, is not bound by possessions,
But by growth, and the joy of life's expressions.

It's not in the wealth that the world may acclaim,
But in the pursuit of dreams, the burning flame.
For success is not measured by what we acquire,
But by the love that sets our souls on fire.

Find solace in moments that make your heart sing,
In the laughter and love that each day can bring.
Seek not the approval of others' desires,
But let your own dreams be the fuel that inspires.

Embrace the uniqueness that lies deep within,
For it's in being yourself that true success begins.

In every endeavor, let passion ignite,
And watch as your spirit takes glorious flight.
So chase your dreams, my dear one, with all your might,
And let your heart guide you through darkest night.
For success is not found in the world's acclaim,
But in the journey that leaves your soul forever changed.

TWENTY-FOUR

YOU'LL FIND TRUE SUCCESS

In the realm of dreams, where possibilities reside,
A soul yearns to soar, to the highest heights.
With every step taken, a path unveiled,
Success awaits, with stories yet untold.

Through valleys of doubt, and mountains steep,
Comes the call to rise, from a slumber deep.
Embrace the failures, the stumbling blocks,
For they carve the path, where triumph knocks.

Success, dear friend, is not defined,
By accolades and laurels, left behind.
It's found in the moments, oh so small,
Where passion ignites and hearts enthrall.

Trust in your journey, let it guide,
For destiny knows where stars reside.

Embrace uncertainties, dance with fears,
And in the face of doubt, let courage appear.
Seek not the measure, the world's acclaim,
But the joy that comes, from playing the game.
For in the pursuit of dreams, lies the key,
To finding success, in being authentically free.
So let your spirit soar, with wings unfurled,
And let the fire within, light up your world.
With every step, every try, every setback,
You'll find strength anew, and dreams intact.
For success, my dear, is not an end,
But a journey of growth, a message to send.
Embrace it with passion, with love and zest,
And in the pursuit of dreams, you'll find true success.

TWENTY-FIVE

DAY BY DAY

In the realm of dreams, where passion dwells,
A story of success, a tale that compels.
Not bound by limits, nor weighed by doubt,
A journey of growth, that's what it's about.
Success is not measured by wealth or fame,
But by the fire that burns within, aflame.
It's the pursuit of dreams, where hearts align,
A symphony of purpose, a destiny divine.
With every step forward, new horizons unfold,
Unveiling treasures, untold and untold.
Through valleys of challenges, we find our way,
Gathering strength, growing, day by day.
Success is the blossoming of a resilient soul,
Nurtured by setbacks, making us whole.
It's the courage to rise, after every fall,
A testament of character, standing tall.

So let not the fear of failure hold you back,
Embrace the unknown, let your spirit unpack.
For success lies not in the destination alone,
But in the journey, the growth we have known.
Follow your passion, let it be your guide,
With every endeavor, let your heart be your pride.
For in the pursuit of dreams, we find true success,
A life well-lived, a story to impress.

TWENTY-SIX

GOALS YOU PURSUE

In a world consumed by riches and fame,
Success is often defined by earthly gain.
But let me tell you, dear friend, a different tale,
Where success is found in a different trail.
　　It's not in the numbers on your bank account,
Or the possessions you flaunt, there's no amount.
True success lies in the growth you embrace,
In the passion that sets your soul ablaze.
　　Success is found in the lessons you learn,
In the bridges you build, the bridges you burn.
It's in the knowledge you gain, the wisdom you share,
In the moments of triumph, the moments of despair.
　　Success is not a race, nor a finish line,
But a journey of purpose, a story divine.
It's in the dreams you chase, the goals you pursue,
In the actions you take, in the choices you choose.

So let go of comparison, let go of the crowd,
Find your own voice, let it ring out loud.
For success is not defined by the world's decree,
But by the person you become, the person you see.
Embrace your uniqueness, embrace your own light,
For success is found in the depths of your might.
So follow your heart, let passion be your guide,
And success will be yours, side by side.
For in the end, my dear friend, you'll come to see,
That true success is being authentically free.
Not bound by others' expectations and strife,
But living a life that's true to your life.
So go forth, my friend, and chase your own dreams,
For success is not as it always seems.
It's in the joy you find, the love you give,
In the life you create, the way you live.

TWENTY-SEVEN

SUCCESS IS NOT A DESTINATION

In the realm of dreams, where magic resides,
There lies a path that only you can stride.
Embrace your uniqueness, let it shine bright,
For success is found in your own guiding light.
Unleash your passions, let them take flight,
Reach for the stars with all your might.
In the pursuit of dreams, you shall prevail,
For in your heart, the seeds of success never fail.
Break free from the chains that hold you down,
Rise above the noise, wear your own crown.
The road less traveled may be rough and tough,
But it's in the challenges that you'll find enough.
Success is not a destination, but a wondrous quest,
A journey of growth, where you are truly blessed.

Embrace each setback, learn from every fall,
For they are the stepping stones to conquer it all.
 Remember, dear soul, your worth is defined,
Not by the world's acclaim or others' design.
Success is found in being authentically free,
In becoming the person you're meant to be.
 So dream big, my friend, and never lose sight,
For success is found in your own inner light.
Embrace your uniqueness, let it guide your way,
And watch as your dreams unfold, day by day.

TWENTY-EIGHT

PASSION SO FIERCE

In the depths of our hearts, a fire ignites,
A spark that fuels our dreams and ignites,
A passion so fierce, it consumes our soul,
A longing for success, our ultimate goal.
But success, dear friend, is not in fame,
Nor in worldly acclaim or a name.
It's found in the love that sets our souls on fire,
In the moments of joy that never tire.
Success is the laughter that fills the air,
The love that we give and the love that we share.
It's in the kindness we show, day by day,
In the helping hand we offer along the way.
Success is not measured by riches or gold,
But by the stories we tell and the lives we mold.
It's in the lessons we learn, the wisdom we gain,
In the strength we find when we face the pain.

So, chase your dreams with unwavering might,
Embrace the darkness and seek the light.
For success is not a destination to be won,
But a journey of growth, where we become one.

TWENTY-NINE

STRIVE FOR SUCCESS EACH DAY

In love we find the key to soar,
To heights we've never known before.
Success is not in wealth or fame,
But in the fire that sets our souls aflame.
In moments of joy that never tire,
We find the fuel to reach higher.
For success is not in what we gain,
But in the love we give, and not in vain.
In the laughter that fills our days,
In the embrace that lights our ways.
Success is not a destination to seek,
But a journey where love and joy we speak.
For in the depths of our heart's desire,
Success is found in love's eternal fire.

In every smile we bring to another's face,
In every warm embrace, we find our grace.
So let us strive for success each day,
Not in the trophies or worldly display.
But in the love we share, the joy we bring,
Success is found in the song we sing.

THIRTY

DETERMINATION AND UNWAVERING FAITH

In the face of challenges, we find our strength,
For it is in adversity that we truly grow.
Success is not in accolades, nor in wealth,
But in the journey of becoming, we come to know.
    Embrace the hurdles that come your way,
For they shape the path to your destiny.
With determination and unwavering faith,
You'll conquer mountains, no matter how steep.
    Success is not a destination, but a state of mind,
A reflection of the person you choose to be.
It's not about comparisons or societal norms,
But about finding your own authenticity.
    Find joy in the process, in every step you take,

For each moment is a chance to learn and evolve.
Don't be afraid to stumble, for in failure lies a gift,
A chance to rise again, stronger and resolved.

Success is not measured by external gains,
But by the love and joy we bring to others' lives.
So, chase your dreams with passion and purpose,
And let your inner light shine, like a thousand fire-
flies.

In the pursuit of success, remember this truth,
It's not about what you achieve, but who you become.
Embrace the challenges, embrace your unique self,
And success will be yours, forever and beyond.

THIRTY-ONE

FAR AND WIDE

In the realm of dreams, where magic lies,
A spark of fire, a soul that flies.
With every beat, a rising tide,
A journey beckons, far and wide.
Success, my friend, is not defined,
By trophies won or wealth assigned.
It's in the laughter, in the tears,
In overcoming all our fears.
Resilience, like a warrior's shield,
In the face of doubt, it will not yield.
For every stumble, every fall,
We rise again, standing tall.
Authenticity, our guiding light,
Unveiling truths, shining bright.
Embrace your quirks, your flaws, your grace,
For there lies beauty, in every trace.

Challenges, they shape our soul,
Revealing strengths we never know.
Embrace them all, with open arms,
For growth and learning, they're the charms.
And in this journey, let us find,
The joy that's nestled in our mind.
Not just in reaching lofty goals,
But in the love that fills our souls.
Success is not a distant land,
But a dance of life, hand in hand.
So let us chase our dreams, my friend,
And find success, until the end.

THIRTY-TWO

YOUR OWN MISSION

In a world that thrives on imitation,
Where success seems like a fixed equation,
I urge you to seek your own liberation,
And embrace a path of innovation.

For success is not a mere replication,
But a journey filled with determination,
It's about finding your true vocation,
And making a mark with your creation.

Unleash the power of your imagination,
Break free from the chains of limitation,
Discover your truest inspiration,
And create a life of endless fascination.

Success lies not in chasing validation,
But in the joy of self-realization,
Find your purpose with dedication,
And let your unique light shine without hesitation.

Remember, success is not a competition,
It's a celebration of your own rendition,
It's about finding joy in the process of transition,
And making a difference with your own mission.
So, dare to dream, dare to be bold,
Embrace the challenges that unfold,
For success, my friend, is not bought or sold,
But in the love and joy your journey beholds.

THIRTY-THREE

SELF-DISCOVERY

In the depths of doubt, where shadows loom,
A spark of fire, within you, blooms.
Embrace the challenge, don't shy away,
For it is through struggle, you find your way.
Success is not a prize to be won,
But a journey, cherished, once begun.
It's not in accolades or worldly fame,
But in the love and joy you bring, your flame.
Embrace the failures, they are your guide,
Opportunities to learn and grow, beside.
For in each stumble, a lesson unfolds,
And strength is found in stories untold.
Dance with passion, sing with all your might,
Let your heart's desires be your guiding light.
For success is not defined by others' norms,
But by the authenticity that your soul adorns.

Follow your dreams, with unwavering grace,
And let your unique talents leave a trace.
For in the pursuit of truth, you will find,
A life well-lived, and peace of mind.

So, dear friend, let go of fear's tight hold,
Embrace the challenges, let your story unfold.
For success is not a destination to be found,
But a journey of self-discovery, profound.

THIRTY-FOUR

LET YOUR IMAGINATION SOAR

In the depths of your soul, a flame does ignite,
A spark that burns bright, with a purpose so right.
A journey awaits, with challenges untold,
To conquer your fears, and let your story unfold.

Success, my dear friend, is not in gold or fame,
But in the joy you bring, when you play your own game.
Embrace your uniqueness, let your colors shine,
For success is found in being authentically thine.

Embrace the failures, the stumbles, the falls,
For they are the lessons that sculpt your walls.
In each setback, there lies a hidden treasure,
A chance to grow stronger, beyond any measure.

Find your passion, your calling, your bliss,
And let it guide you through the abyss.

Dream big, my love, let your imagination soar,
For success is found in dreams explored.
Celebrate your flaws, for they make you whole,
They shape your character, they touch your soul.
Success is not a destination, my dear,
But a journey of growth, year after year.
So rise up, my friend, and chase your dreams high,
With love as your compass, reaching for the sky.
Success is yours, in the making each day,
Believe in yourself, and you'll find your own way.

THIRTY-FIVE

A JOURNEY OF GROWTH

In a world of infinite possibilities, where dreams take flight,
A soul seeks success, with all its might.
But what is success, if not a journey of its own,
To find joy in the process, and let one's light be shown.

Embrace the challenges that come your way,
For they mold you into who you are today.
In every stumble and fall, there lies a lesson,
To rise again, with passion and obsession.

Be true to yourself, for that's where the magic lies,
Unleash your imagination, and watch it mesmerize.
Break free from limitations, let your spirit soar,
Create a life of endless fascination, forevermore.

Success is not a validation, nor a competition to

win,
It's about self-realization, and the joy found within.
Make a difference, touch lives with your own mission,
Leave a mark on the world, with love and ambition.

Dare to dream, and let your heart take the lead,
Embrace the challenges, they're what you need.
Celebrate your own rendition of success,
For it's a reflection of your uniqueness, no less.

Success cannot be bought or sold,
It's the love, joy, and growth that unfold.
With dedication and purpose, you'll find your way,
To make a difference, and brighten someone's day.

So, follow your heart, and seek peace of mind,
In the pursuit of truth and self-discovery, you'll find,
That success is not a destination, but a state of being,
A journey of growth, and a life worth seeing.

ABOUT THE AUTHOR

Walter the Educator is one of the pseudonyms for Walter Anderson. Formally educated in Chemistry, Business, and Education, he is an educator, an author, a diverse entrepreneur, and he is the son of a disabled war veteran. "Walter the Educator" shares his time between educating and creating. He holds interests and owns several creative projects that entertain, enlighten, enhance, and educate, hoping to inspire and motivate you.

Follow, find new works, and stay up to date
with Walter the Educator™
at WaltertheEducator.com